A MATH SAFARI

Greater Than, Less Than, and Equal To

by Joanne Randolph

STECK-VAUGHN

 Harcourt Supplemental Publishers

www.steck-vaughn.com

Let's go on a math safari!
Compare the groups of animals you see.
Here are two groups of birds.

Is the first group of birds
> **<** **=**
greater than, **less than**, or **equal to**
the second group?

>

3 birds **is greater than** 2 birds.

A rhinoceros has a horn and a very tough hide.
The baby stays close to its mother's side.
Compare the two groups—don't just guess.
Does the first group of rhinos have more or less?

Choose **greater than**, **less than**, or **equal to**.
That is all you have to do.
Think it through with all your might.
Then check to see if you are right!

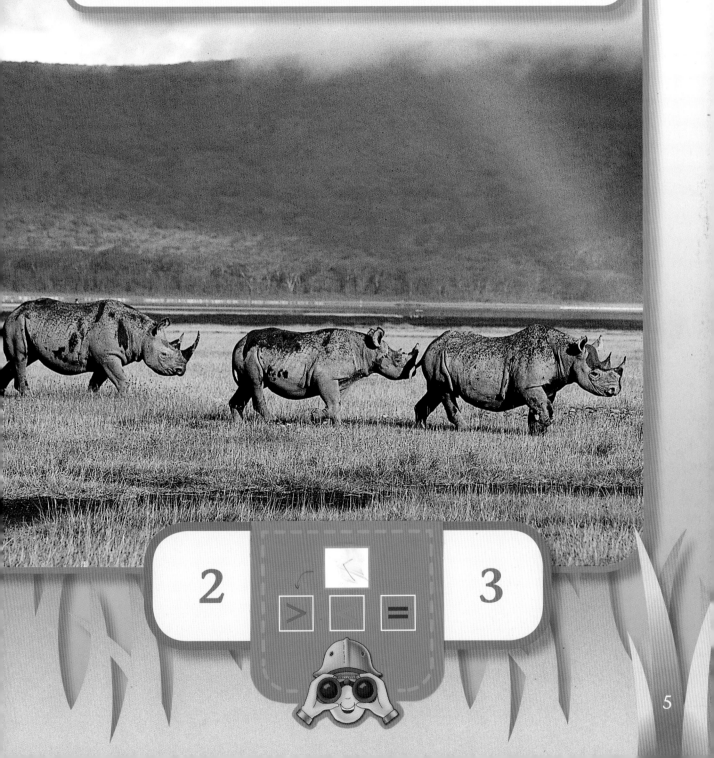

2   > □ =   3

Young chimpanzees like to play.
They often have a lot to say.
Compare the two groups—don't just guess.
Does the first group of chimps have more or less?

Choose **greater than**, **less than**, or **equal to**.
That is all you have to do.
Think it through with all your might.
Then check to see if you are right!

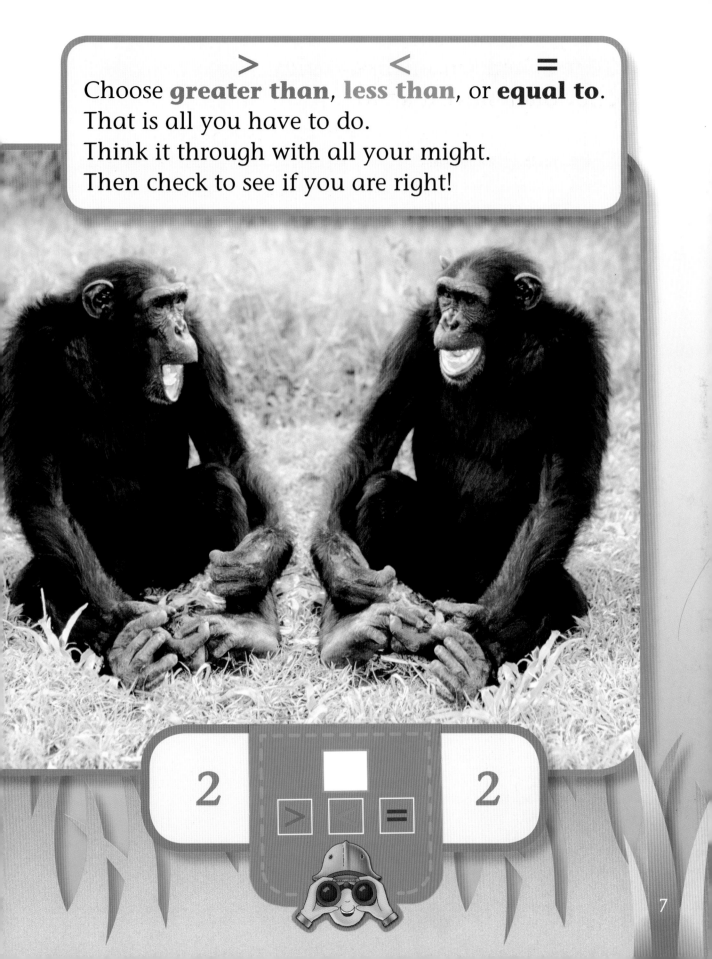

2   2

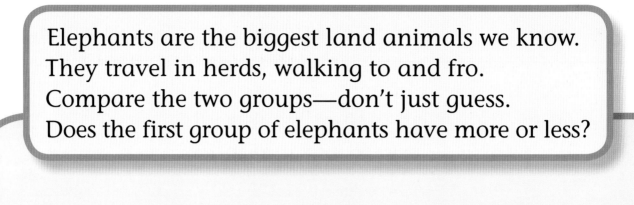

Elephants are the biggest land animals we know.
They travel in herds, walking to and fro.
Compare the two groups—don't just guess.
Does the first group of elephants have more or less?

>   <   =

Choose **greater than**, **less than**, or **equal to**.
That is all you have to do.
Think it through with all your might.
Then check to see if you are right!

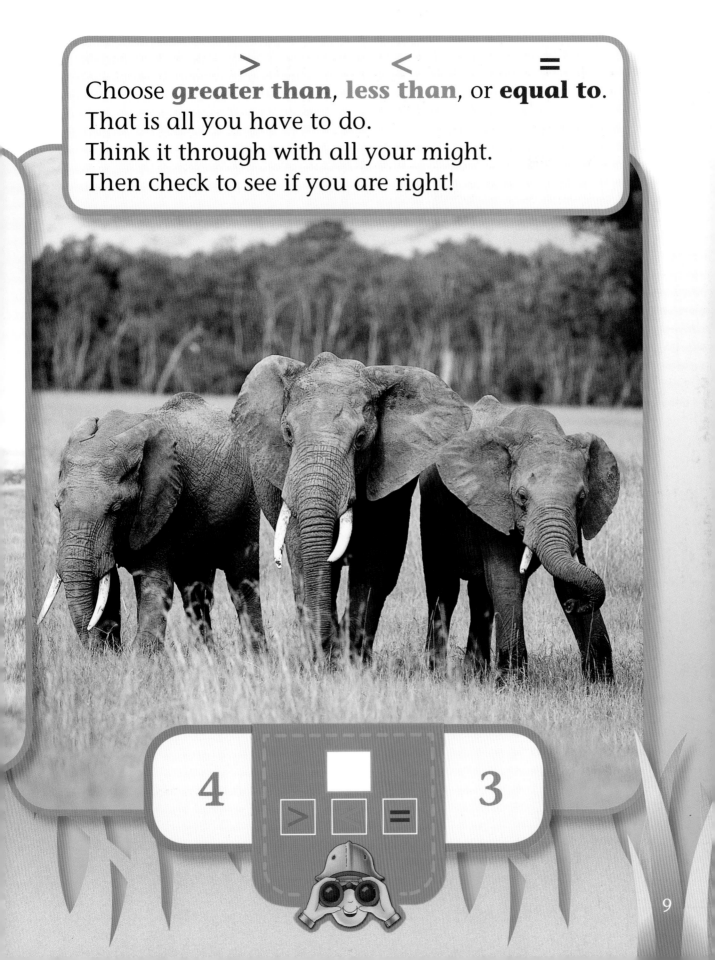

4   >   <   =   3

A group of lions is called a pride.
These big cats travel far and wide.
Compare the two groups—don't just guess.
Does the first group of lions have more or less?

Choose **greater than** >, **less than** <, or **equal to** =.
That is all you have to do.
Think it through with all your might.
Then check to see if you are right!

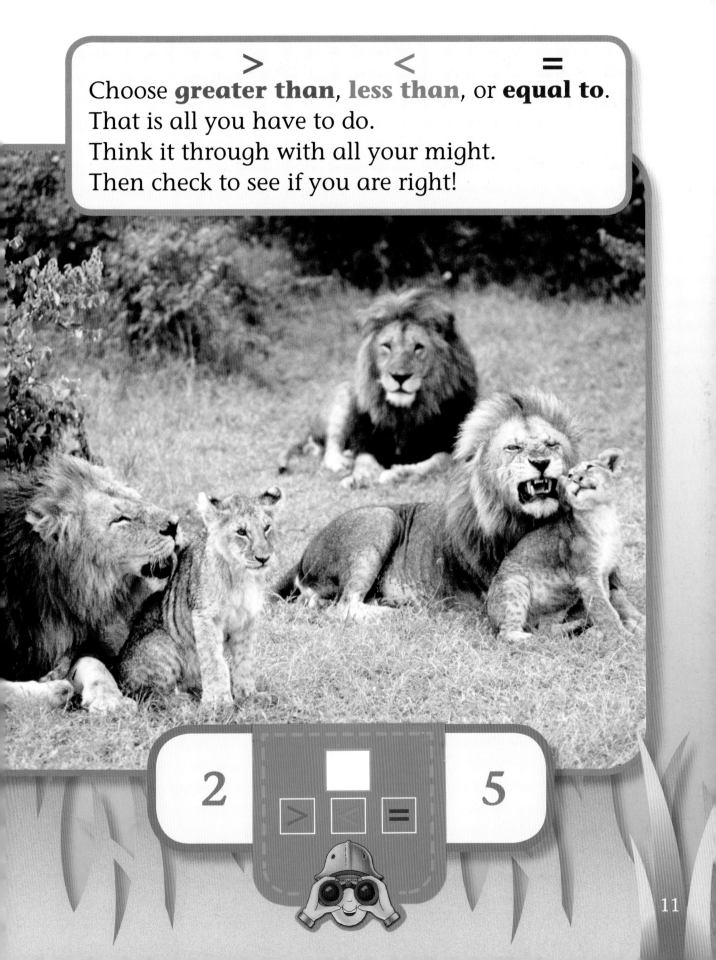

2 ☐ 5

> < =

Giraffes are the tallest animals around.
They can reach the treetops from the ground!
Compare the two groups—don't just guess.
Does the first group of giraffes have more or less?

Choose **greater than**, **less than**, or **equal to**.
That is all you have to do.
Think it through with all your might.
Then check to see if you are right!

> < =

6   3

> [ ] =

13

Some hippos swim in the water for fun.
Others like to lie in the sun.
Compare the two groups—don't just guess.
Does the first group of hippos have more or less?

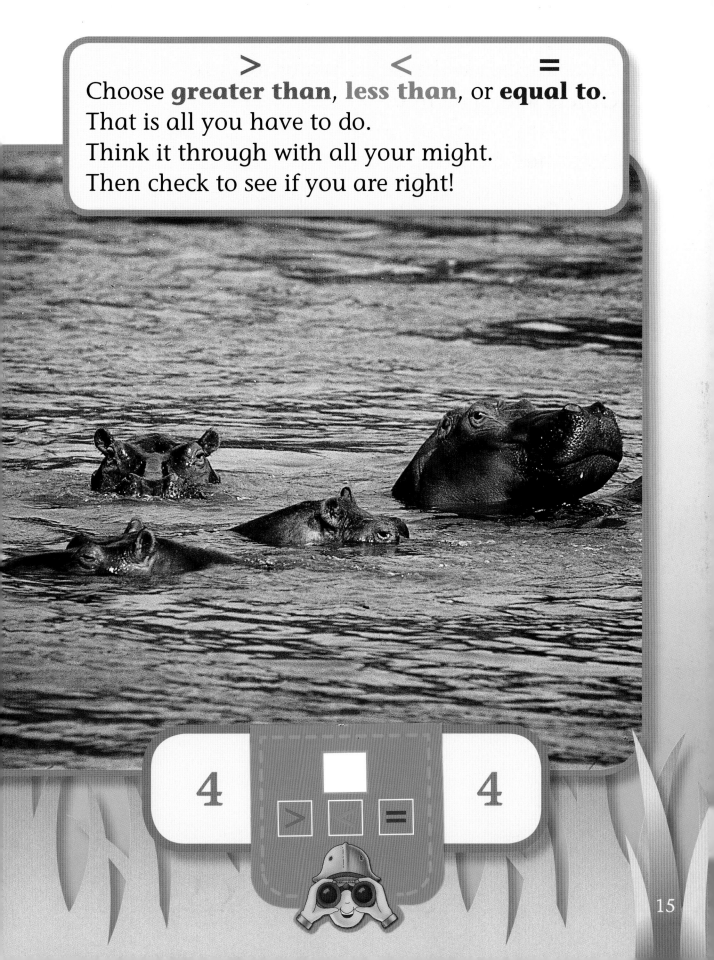

Choose **greater than**, **less than**, or **equal to**.
That is all you have to do.
Think it through with all your might.
Then check to see if you are right!

4 ☐ 4

> < =

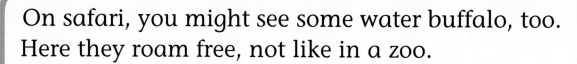

On safari, you might see some water buffalo, too.
Here they roam free, not like in a zoo.
Compare the two groups—don't just guess.
Does the first group of water buffalo have more or less?

Choose **greater than**, **less than**, or **equal to**.
That is all you have to do.
Think it through with all your might.
Then check to see if you are right!

6 ▢ 1

> ◁ =

Impalas will jump at the smallest sound.
They can leap ten feet straight off the ground!
Compare the two groups—don't just guess.
Does the first group of impalas have more or less?

Choose **greater than**, **less than**, or **equal to**.
That is all you have to do.
Think it through with all your might.
Then check to see if you are right!

3   > < =   7

Zebras have stripes of black and white.
A herd of these animals is quite a sight.
Compare the two groups—don't just guess.
Does the first group of zebras have more or less?

Choose **greater than**, **less than**, or **equal to**.
That is all you have to do.
Think it through with all your might.
Then check to see if you are right!

5   ☐   5

\>   <   =

Ostriches are birds that cannot fly.
They run so fast, they zoom right by!
Compare the two groups—don't just guess.
Does the first group of ostriches have more or less?

Choose **greater than**, less than, or **equal to**.
That is all you have to do.
Think it through with all your might.
Then check to see if you are right!

4 □ 6

> < =

Our math safari has come to an end.
But you can take the trip again with a friend!
Start over at the beginning, you know what to do.

>   <   =

Choose **greater than**, **less than**, or **equal to**.